Dedicated with thanks to Lesley Sutton
for your encouragement and inspiration.

First published in Great Britain in 2021

Instant Apostle,
The Barn,
Watford House Lane,
Watford, Herts
WD17 1BJ

Other books by the author:
Time to Live: The Beginner's Guide
to Saying Goodbye
Where is God in Our 21st Century world?

British Library Cataloguing-in-Publication Data

A catalogue record for this book is available
from the British Library

This book and all other Instant Apostle books are
available from Instant Apostle:
www.instantapostle.com
E-mail: info@instantapostle.com

Chaiya Art Awards
www.chaiyaartawards.co.uk
E-mail: info@chaiyaartawards.co.uk
Registered charity: Chaiya Trust 1176237.

ISBN 978-1-912726-23-3
Printed in Great Britain

ANN CLIFFORD

GOD IS...

contents

a prayer

'My God, my God ... You are a figurative, a metaphorical God ... a God in whose words there is such a height of figures, such voyages ... to fetch remote and precious metaphors, such extensions, such spreadings, such curtains of allegories ... and such things in your words ... you are the Dove that flies.'

John Donne
Devotions (alt. to reflect modern English)[1]

FOREWORD: GIFT

feel tremendously privileged to present the artwork and writing contained here to everyone who buys or receives a copy of book two in this series.

Lives have altered in so many ways with the arrival of COVID-19, and it has thrown us into unknown territory within ourselves.

The upended society in which we now live raises many internal questions.

Today it is even more important to give voice to diverse creative expressions on a subject key to many – their spirituality. The varied artwork in this book represents a hand-picked selection of the 700+ artists who entered these awards on the theme 'God is…' Some share my faith, some come from different faith backgrounds, some are exploring the subject and others have no faith at all, but each artist has shared their imagination, their creative talent and their unique response to this theme.

As you rest awhile with each piece and the thought-provoking poetry and prose which accompanies each section, my heartfelt prayer is that you will encounter the God who knows you, loves you and waits to reveal the mysteries of life, love, pain, suffering and joy.

From all at Chaiya Art Awards, this is our gift to you.

CHAIYA TRUST

Katrina Moss, Founder, Chaiya Art Awards

LANDSCAPE

In 2020, our world changed.

For many it became a world of lamentation, fear, separation, anxiety, social distancing, economic depression, need, loneliness, mental and emotional distress, uncertainty, disruption, debilitating illness and widening social and racial divide. For others a world of pause, time 'to be', communing with nature, learning fresh skills, becoming the fittest we had ever been, a fresh and grateful renewed perspective on family and relationships. For some, their job brought them to unknown depths of fatigue. For others, their job became hazardous. Those who delivered to our homes, drove emergency vehicles, deep-cleaned premises, became vital. Together in 2021 we survey an irreversibly altered landscape as the spectre of COVID-19 remains, affecting not only our country but also our planet.

A sphere of noise and time-struggle straddled our activities before lockdowns peppered our lives. Lockdown separated siblings, grandparents, extended family, children, grandchildren, lovers and friends, and we complied, wanting deliverance from all in this uncharted territory, despite its underlying cruelty. In the first lockdown kindness mushroomed – when the NHS (National Health Service, UK) asked for volunteers to augment their services, 400,000 of us stepped up. Neighbour discovered neighbour, and help was on hand. A testament to a hidden culture that cared. Family, in its broadest sense, highlighted connection and amplified disconnection. A third lockdown, occurring just before and continuing over Christmas and into the New Year, found a nation wearied.

Fissures of inequality and poverty opened, increasing need for foodbanks and meals for children. Perhaps the greatest illumination occurred in racial inequality; angry voices against endemic racism and questions about the disproportionality of Blacks and Asians dying from the disease.

Governments struggled to find clarity and perspective amid the overwhelming scientific data. Their task? To navigate a pathway of wisdom through a catastrophe most global leaders were ill prepared for. We will nurse and rehearse the story of the pandemic over decades, but one thing we recognise, the decimation of 2020, leaching into 2021, ongoing until vaccination takes full effect, will reveal itself as devastating as war. Its seismic eruption must affect our children, our children's children, and beyond. May they forgive us for the havoc wrought through our many failures.

'Today, in a world full of conflict and shocks, art bears witness to the most precious part of what makes us human … At a time of global disorder, art embraces life.'

Christine Macel[2]

For some, a touch of myopia in this unprecedented time permitted us to leave in order to return as we sought nourishment for our heart and soul and spirit in the natural world. For others, the anaesthetising properties of filling our lives with online entertainment soon left a dissatisfying emptiness. We wanted to eat, chew, swallow and digest that which nourished our well-being.

This theme-based competition is food for the soul, worthwhile to devour, devoted as it is to addressing a higher consciousness; to travel a path of wonder; to seek the immaterial mystery of the numinous or 'Spirit'.

In the silence and stillness of contemplation we unlock ourselves to fresh experiences, for which, perhaps, we have no language. Pondering God and the concept of His being is heady and surprising. If God is real, then expect Him to reveal Himself.

The artists featured in this book invite us to muse with them about their journey, laying before us a heartland of fullness. They reduce, simplify, purify and attempt to align themselves with that which is beyond complete expression.

Historically, art has narrated stories with relatable images to our story-absorbed history. Some curated images here are figurative; others abstract. Abstract art reaches into uncharted territory, like a wind we cannot see but feel.

The work is a variety of mediums – canvas and paper; photographs; cloth and stitch; 3D metalwork and pottery; bronze and stone sculpture; glass and pipework; a movement-sensitive robot alongside an interactive sign with sonic sensors. All the pieces cry out for time and patience to mine the artists' ideas.

What does the theme 'God is…' ask? Our understanding of life is individual, but we are all damaged, we all cry out in pain and pleasure, we all crave connection and something more… Grasping the opportunity to explore spirituality will enrich, sustain and offer adventurous hope.

I am the way, the truth and the life.

JESUS IN THE GARDEN OF EDEN

Daphne Stephenson / Acrylic / W: 110 H: 140cm

Inspired by memories as a six-year-old, living in Pakistan, taking my first Holy Communion. I felt honoured to receive Jesus, and hope I have conveyed His extraordinary love, strength and bravery. I remember the lightness and joy I felt in my spirit. This painting depicts wholeness, freedom, peace, joy and rest.

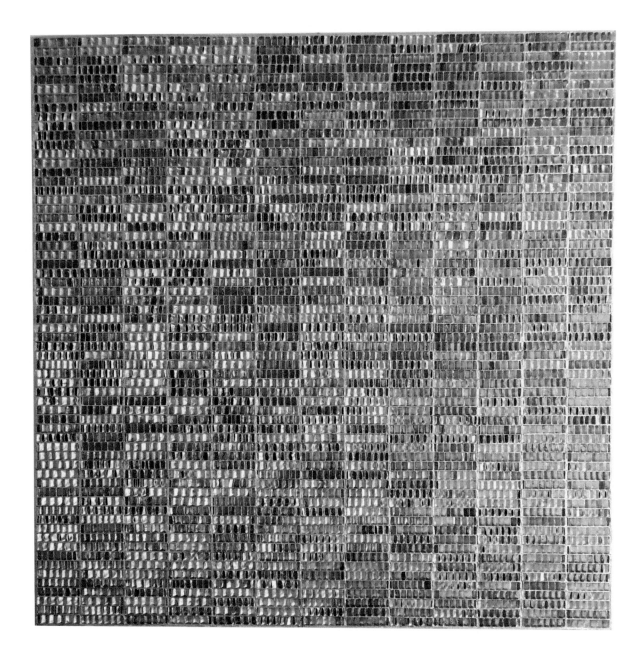

GOLDEN ALGORITHM

Mark Osborne / Gold leaf paints, acrylics on folded cardboard mounted on MDF / W: 117 H: 116cm

The piece is abstract. It deals with materials, surfaces, reflections, shadows, and, because
of its 3D quality, it engages with the light and changes all through the day. This is the stuff
of existence for me.

CONSOLATION

There are times
when we want
to be filled with
something
we cannot
explain; to be
comforted and
stilled; to look
beyond what
can be seen
to explore that
which cannot.

New beginnings

The heart begins a tiny, unformed
wandering craft,
waiting, listening, garnering.
A child-sized information-gatherer
tethered by numerous teachers.

It grows
and weighs anchor.
The mists of seas encircle,
the pleats of darkness blind,
storms gather, batter and becalm.
Within the unquiet soul
arise the ghouls of fear.
Alone
in an unstable boat
it longs to return
to sound harbour,
but its cries, heard,
reveal the secret space
of faith.

As the mist clears,
a new-minted spirit
now navigates
to a different wind called trust –
adventure's tack.

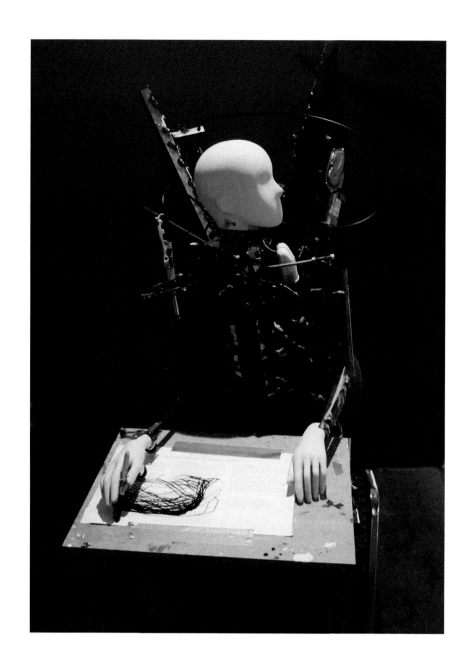

DELETION
Myles Mansfield / Kinetic steel sculpture built from scrap metal / W: 60 H: 200 D: 100cm Weight: 40kg

A robot built from scrap materials that scribbles and destroys my original artwork when alone. When someone enters, it stops and turns its head to look at them. Its chest rises and falls, imitating breathing. It has wings to symbolise our god, 'technology', as the solution to our unhappiness.

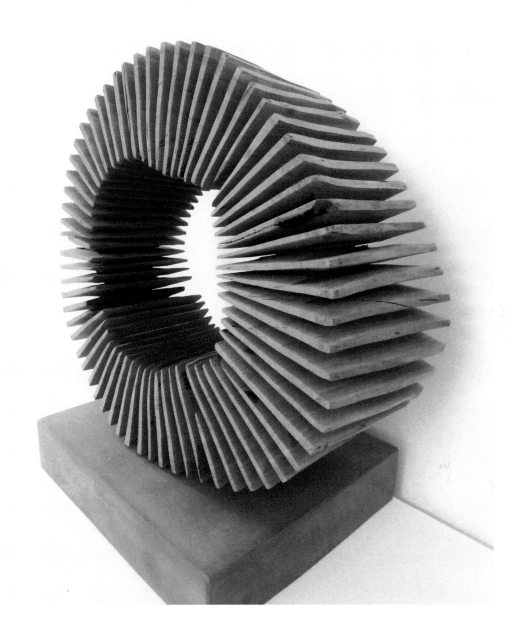

RADIANT
Philippine Sowerby / Local cherry wood from Powys / W: 35 H: 40 D: 22cm with the stone base Weight: 14kg

God is radiant through all of creation living in harmony. A ring made of rays connected
by a central core. We are called to communion with God, and unity not uniformity with all
of humankind. When this happens, God can be present and visible, radiant like the sun,
Light of the World.

i can't breathe

So simple
Life... living... breathing
In two three, out two three
In two three, out two three
Lungs threatened,
Body fouled
By virulence –
Spreading, filling,
Taking,
Sucking life.
Nano second by nano second
Body shelled
And we, the onlookers,
Watch and wait
In fear
For our breath-less intubation.

George Floyd
Another name, another man,
Another emptying.
A human being imaged in the Divine
Like us
A man of dust returned there
By a knee.
How great our shame that
Inalienable rights
Again prove sectioned,
Where white clambers on black
Without mercy.

Two viruses
The difference –
One could be eradicated
By a vaccine.

June 2020

"Not everything
that is faced can
be changed,
but nothing can
be changed until
it is faced."

James Baldwin[3]

another's shoes

When African–American George Floyd died at the hands of the police in Minneapolis, Minnesota, it galvanised an entire Black Lives Matter protest over many parts of the world. Caught on film, on 25 May 2020, white police officer Derek Chauvin pinned George Floyd to the ground by placing his knee on his neck until he died, despite Mr Floyd's repeated cries that he could not breathe. Charged with second- and third-degree murder and manslaughter, the court granted Mr Chauvin bail while awaiting trial. The three other officers present at the incident are also facing charges, and the department has since fired the four officers.

The effect of George Floyd's death has been dramatic among black and diverse ethnicities worldwide. Huge numbers marched against racism in the USA, UK and other countries.

The banner 'Black Lives Matter' encompassed the dynamic world movement which mushroomed in protest. Accompanying these three words, written and spoken many times in multiple ways, are many heart-rending stories of endemic racism.

Listening and learning during COVID uncovered the racism in my own heart, and I recognised I was part of the problem. As a white person speaking to white people, it seems to me we each live our own story into which we place ourselves as hero, which allows us to disregard, dismantle and denigrate any other story that disagrees with ours. If, with humility, we replace ourselves as hero in order to step into the shoes of others to learn, a radical change in us and therefore society becomes possible. If we listen to the heart cries around us, we will understand how vital it is to stand against racism, in all its forms, wherever we find it.

'No-one is born hating another person because of the colour of his skin, or his background, or his religion. People must learn to hate and if they can learn to hate, they can be taught to love, for love comes more naturally to the human heart than its opposite.'

Nelson Mandela[4]

'Jesus and I don't agree on all matters. I can't, for instance, go along with Mr Christ's idea that to think a crime is as bad as to commit one. But when he talks about first taking the great plank of wood out of our own eyes before presuming to criticise the tiny speck in other people's he has a point. So perhaps it might be illuminating, instructive, or at least entertaining to look at something very inward and personal that almost never gets looked at these days. Usually when we look inside we are encouraged to congratulate ourselves on our beautiful, underappreciated and cruelly misunderstood personalities, but I want to take away the jewel encrusted stone of our shining selves and reveal the nasty squirming slimy creatures that crawl beneath – our sins.'

Stephen Fry[5]

Freedom Prayer

God, we stand before you
without shoes.

Shoes are symbolic of the many
things racism has trampled upon

to diminish black women, men
and children in every way.

We have called this world 'ours',
and as 'superior' beings

not accepted the equal
voices of others.

We continue to shun, laugh,
pour scorn, dismiss, incarcerate,
traffic and enslave,

believing we have the right to do so.

We see ourselves as
loftier in every way.

We deride, insult, belittle,
fail to allow space for

each to take their
rightful place, and for all this,

we are ashamed.

Forgive us.

Make a way for truth, reconciliation
and justice to stand in our country.

Change our hearts,

fill us with your humility,

help us root out this accursed sin

in all its diverse forms,

and replace it with a love that is
positive, active

and change-making.

« Detail. See page 30

WHO HAS SEEN THE WIND?

Christy Burdock / Acrylic on canvas / W: 100 H: 150cm

A painting based on a Quaker meeting and its prevailing narratives and discourse. It talks about a poem, 'Who Has Seen the Wind?' by Christina Rossetti that was referred to during 'ministry' by a member of the praying group.

FISH IV #1 THE SEA IS DEEP
Chris Wilmott / Oil on board / W: 50 H: 60cm

The work represents water, air, life and changing climates. It is one of a series exploring the stanza 'the sea is deep and full of fish, but maybe this is not a wish'. It focuses on the first four words. The viewer may ask: are there fish, where are the fish and where are the people? Considering loss is part of the human condition.

living too thinly

Being human

Have we lost the sense of our true identity on this beleaguered planet of ours? We thrash about in a deeply uncomfortable and disturbing soup, the ingredients of which include global conflict and care, beginning and end of life, artificial intelligence, identity politics, immigration and integration, social care for all, economic divisions, internet regulation, tribalism and nationalism, and so much more.

What does it mean to be human? Is this question one of the most contested arenas in our current culture today?

There are so many competing narratives trying to structure and systematise who we are, what constitutes each individual human, and to deliver an understanding of personal identity.

Do we buy our story from the most compelling bidder of the day?

Historically, beginning several centuries ago, the formation of our values in the UK matured from the crucible of Christianity from which the God of the Bible defined the highest view of what it meant to be human. This narrative explained we were made in His image. God endowed great dignity and honour, unearned by us, to His human creation. Unpacking this endowment included dwelling on this earth, contributing to all through an active loving, a sacrificial living, a commitment to reconciliation, a positive nourishing of both the community of fellow human beings and our physical environment – our world. Many initiatives for the good of the poor, anti-slavery, etc, were begun because of this narrative.

As Peter Lynas and Jo Frost say in their article 'Being Human',[6] 'we are "storied" creatures'. If we bend without question to the strongest story, our own narrative about our humanity will disintegrate as we trust one imperfect storyteller after another. Deprived of genuine substance and sustenance, our lives become thin and friable.

Do we need the sustenance of certainty? Can ongoing cohesion and harmony reside without it? Derided absolutes founded on a personal God who became human and walked the earth have become transportable, malleable values and beliefs. Have we lost everything, been stripped naked and left quivering in our vulnerability?

Into whose storied hands would we place ourselves? Which hands do we trust to hold us as a newborn baby, expressing a parent's heart of love and unequivocal self-sacrifice?

Whether we believe in God or not, many of us long to mark-make somewhere, somehow in our society. To leave a remembrance of ourselves, to not be forgotten. This deep-rooted desire perhaps draws on a profound sense within us that we were born as a human being for a purpose. It unsettles, jostles and discombobulates. What that purpose is might be as mysterious as the depths of the ocean, but does not invalidate the sense. It is like the desire for eternity exemplified by the Elon Musks of this world and their pursuit, through artificial intelligence, to conquer death, the final frontier.

Consciously or unconsciously we are all guided by a story or stories. Being human – which story do we choose to live?

'God is dead, that I cannot deny. But that my whole being cries out for God: that I can never forget.'

Jean-Paul Sartre

SHELTER
Rachel Ho / Porcelain paper clay (ceramics) / W: 8 H: 13cm each shelter Weight 100g

Each porcelain paper clay shelter is embossed with an old Irish proverb, alongside its translation, 'It is in the shelter of each other that the people live.' Each imperfect shelter is glazed with gold lustre on the cracks and tears, speaking of new beginnings and renewal. Shelter is solace, hope and transformation. John O'Donohue reminds, 'in the kindest of care, the divine comes alive in us'.

GOD

Jo Fairfax / Acrylic, MDF, sonic sensors and Arduino / W: 63 H: 44 D: 10cm Weight: 24kg

'GOD' is a result of my considering the position of God in relation to a mechanical universe. I have been wondering about this question for the past forty years and this is my first artwork about the topic.

INTERSECTION

Perhaps God is nearer than we think.

Perhaps He intersects our lives in the everyday minutiae of life.

A God whose presence is like a fine thread of gold woven through everything.

A thread that can be touched wherever we find ourselves.

the cynic

Wet,
freed from the broken birth sac
I kick, cry and howl.
I am alive.
Am I wanted, loved, kissed,
embraced, enfolded?

What happened?
Why?

Why not, I think, now grown.
Experience pushed back –
time burned my edges –
and they withered.
My growth not green,
but brown and ossified.

Hope – that hollow, dreamy,
glass-eyed imposter;
the promoter of rigged ballots;
the artful believer in the improbable
and impossible;
the champion of fake humanity –
proved worthless.

I see the landscape,
from the hollow of my unfilled heart.
Trust I expose in all its weakness –
burn its bridges,
hem its overflowing,
eradicate its compromise,
escalate conflict.

Believe me,
life is betrayal
I own,
my dear,
alone.

the choice

He stands there, this dark-haired tiny person, two-and-a-half years old, his serious chocolate-brown eyes liquid with intent. I have given him a choice, and he has made an important decision.

'Train,' he says.

This means a walk upstairs, with him accompanying me, holding my hand, to the room where various toys have now gathered, owing to my delight in my first grandchild. His old-person noises of exertion accompany his every step. The large, boxed, gold-mining-themed train set gathered into my arms, we make our way downstairs amid much chattering.

'Where is Thomas?'

'In the box with your other train.'

'Where is it?'

'In the box.' He looks up at me with the biggest grin and I respond with my own. Just walking together brings unexpected joys.

'Granny, hold my hand.'

He jumps the final step alone. 'Baby parkour. Well done,' I say. Another winning grin.

He chooses the layout of the large track. I begin with the core of the construction, the tallest piece, with a tunnel representing a large rock. I create the bridge through the rock and attach the gradients, which descend either side of the bridge. Without warning, he places Thomas on the slope alongside the original train attached to an open carriage to carry the plastic rocks. Under these difficult conditions, trains moving on every piece of track I lay, I solemnly continue to follow the diagram, my speed much improved by practice.

He manoeuvres the trains around the track, chattering to himself and the trains, 'Come on, Thomas, you can do it,' as Thomas makes his way up the hill.

His delight is tangible, his interest complete. I sit beside the track on the mats which it had been built on for his comfort (and mine).

'No, Granny. I need the space.'

I move into a chair, pick up a morning coffee and watch him. Everything in this created world captures his imagination. He loves the fact that I am there watching while he plays. Occasionally he lifts his head and smiles, or makes some comment. I offer a drink but he's too absorbed. I place it within the structure. His hand reaches out, he drinks and replaces it. Time passes in the quiet. Every so often I glance out of the window into the garden and see birds feeding, squirrels foraging.

Companionship – an underrated aspiration.

I think of that biblical story of creation, Adam and Eve and God's simple desire for companionship. He loved them and revelled in walking and talking with them.

Companionship – an unacknowledged need.

SHELTER IN THE TIME OF STORMS

Brian Ord / Digital print , oil paint and resin, on canvas, from collage / W: 104 H: 88cm

A visual interpretation of the new Jerusalem being created after a modern-day deluge –
with thanks to William Blake.

SIMPLY WAITING, SIMPLY LOVING
Paul Wadsworth / Oil on canvas / W: 154 H: 117cm

An oil painting about our spiritual relationship to nature, from travels in southern India. A lady waits by a boat for her husband to return with the catch. Often a meagre catch but the family eats well in simple accommodation with simple needs that nature/God has provided. What brings peace, what brings happiness to the family?

sorry

He waits
as he has always waited.
Now it is unconscious
but it was not always so.
At first the pain seared his soul,
bent his back,
every step radiated
grunts of affliction.

Seven years since the parting,
the space called 'son' remained,
unchanged, empty.

Living shrouds the loss,
Nature's springs and summers
saturate time;
the new overshadows,
the old normal recedes.

The empty road stretched,
bringing many travellers,
and longing,
still keened in him
without warning.

The man spied
a strange, distant figure
and breath-denied pining
burst within.
But his attention was diverted
by the new word – 'grandpa' –
uttered at his feet.
His heart returned to its
thankful rhythm
as toddler cheeks
imprinted his own
with cherubic loveliness.

He glanced again at the
unkempt figure
who stooped and hobbled,
and shuddered for breath.
Watched as the lowered
frayed head
faltered and howled.

Recognition like adrenaline
powered limbs,
propelled elbows,
accelerated motion.
Arms stretched wide
to hold and enfold
the mewling and puling.

'My son... my son... my son...'
At each cry of recognition
the other moaned.
Legs faltered and yet
he was held.
A waterfall of tears
cascaded down the embracer's
neck.
Knees crashed to the ground
but still love gripped the broken
boy.

S-s-sorry...
Hush.
Sorry...
Sshh.
Sorry, I...
I love you.

Joy and sorrow's tears mingled
as time emptied.
Rising as one,
they limped together,
home.

« Detail. See page 69

UNSEEN

Sinead Attwell / Oil / W: 120 H: 105cm

God is unseen, therefore is 'He' real? Does that mean 'He' does not exist? Other unexplainable things exist, like the illness ME. This figurative study is of a close friend with ME who fought scepticism and disbelief and sought solace in her relationship with God whom she believes healed her. Depicted here as caught between corporeal existence and enlightenment.

IN THE DETAIL

Stephanie Sandercock / Acrylic and gold leaf on wooden panel / W: 120 H: 120cm

In the beginning was the Word, and the Word was God (John 1:1, NIV). The painting shows a sound wave of the spoken word – God is in the detail. Our world of duality looks black and white but the grey, the gap between, reveals a crack of hope, space for understanding, for unity.

ALPHA AND OMEGA

Larain Briggs / Oils over acrylic underpainting on stretched canvas / H: 100 D: 100cm

Originally this emanated from concern with climate change and the precarious state the natural world is in at present. Although I perceived it to be a vision of the end, it is full of light and hope. It occurred to me that it could equally be the beginning. God is… creation.

ENTANGLEMENT

There is an inter-connectedness of life on this planet that calls for compassion and solidarity. We are all of equal value, despite our many differences, and perhaps should accept each other and work for our corporate well-being and that of our world. Likewise, the spiritual is wrapped around us and through us. God did not separate Himself from us, but lived with us, broke Himself for us and showed us 'home'.

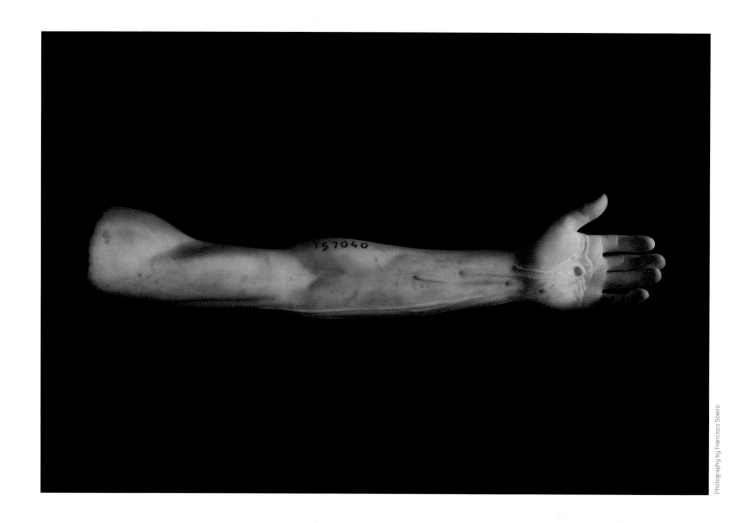

RECONCILIATION
Emma Elliott / Carrara marble / W: 110 H: 20 D: 25cm Weight 50kg

Reconciliation reflects on the connection between atrocities past and present. Through the careful arrangement of iconic imagery, the project confronts the contemporary overexposure and indifference to conflict and brutality when we forget our humanity and live without empathy. 'Do not forget, and this we should shout to the world every day in order to be heard', Eliezer Goldwyn (1922–2017), Holocaust survivor (from Emma's interview with Eliezer Goldwyn).

LIGHT AT THE END OF THE TUNNEL

Tony Tanner / Stainless steel scrapyard finds, cut, machined, welded and polished, combined with electronic and electro-mechanical devices, sensors, actuators and control elements. Incorporating an integral plinth – MDF + paint, with power supply / W: 75 H: 205 D: 65cm Weight: 100kg

This sculpture embodies four ideas: 'God is light' (1 John 1:5, NIV); 'Light at the end of the tunnel' – a metaphor for hope; Dante Alighieri's *Divine Comedy* (his journey through hell): 'I came to myself within a dark wood where the straightway was lost'; and Hieronymus Bosch's *Ascent of the Blessed* where angels guide a naked corpse into the next world through a tunnel of light.

'If we have
no peace,
it is because
we have
forgotten that
we belong to
each other'

Mother Theresa

She had no choice but to leave. She, her husband and her two children left the home into which they had poured creativity and love; left the lemon tree in the garden they had planted on their marriage, a symbol of their roots and fruitfulness. Their extended family wept at their going, yet accepted their choices. The searing pain ripped through both parties as they separated. They must abandon their small, thriving business with little recompense. Home – a physical place where life had been rich and contented, where everything made sense and she could look her neighbour in the eye. A place where her own hands would welcome and feed the stranger; another's child could be scooped up for the day and cared for; where her husband lifted his head and stood with pride among the menfolk. A place where the vine grew, offering fresh grapes alongside other fruit that graced her table.

The bombs and guns systematically demolishing the city she loved, killing the people she treasured, meant they must leave. A family reduced to nothing except each other. The beginning of a journey that would take two torturous years filled with unimaginable sights, unending anxiety, the flagellation of their self-worth alongside the impotence of powerlessness.

Now she found herself in the UK in front of an official, trying again to explain their story, through an interpreter. How to say everything? Shamed, vulnerable, lost, stick-thin, the traumatised parents laid out their shredded life, hoping someone might help them pick up the pieces.

Faced with an uncertainty beyond understanding or words, they must somehow find a way forward in their powerless reality. How will they leave the pain, sorrow and death behind and move to a new world? Fractured lives frozen in time with no sense of when it will end. They all wear shackles, experience a torture and torment where waiting is the drumbeat of their lives.

Where is the entanglement of the divine? The thread that binds and looses. The embodiment of the unseen that propels us into hope. Perhaps in another's small gesture, a smile, a moment of kindness, acknowledgement of vulnerable brotherhood and sisterhood that tethers us all to each other in tiny moments of tenderness. The opportunity for the rekindling of hope, the divine commodity that releases the desire to overcome and build again.

'We lost our home, which means the familiarity of daily life.

We lost our occupation, which means the confidence that we are of some use in this world.

We lost our language, which means the naturalness of reaction, the simplicity of gestures, the unaffected expression of feeling.'

Hannah Arendt, *We Refugees*

An unprecedented 70.8 million people around the world have been forced from home. Among them are nearly 25.9 million refugees, more than half of whom are under the age of eighteen.

There are also millions of stateless people who have been denied a nationality and access to basic rights such as education, healthcare, employment and freedom of movement.

Nearly one person is forcibly displaced every two seconds as a result of conflict or persecution.[7]

GOD IS — THE REST

Jennifer Bell / Oils / W: 66 H: 86cm

An image with a number of layers of meaning: movement towards 'ultimate rest', 'resting' in the arms of the ocean. Is this resting man 'The Rest' or separate...? And there is the notion of sacrifice; in the blood there is life... in the ocean there is now blood.

MOTHER & CHILD
Jo Scorah / Oil on canvas / W: 100 H: 100cm

God is... The power to be omnipresent. Acceptance. Hanging by a thread. Wrapped around us. The inspiration was the expulsion of Syrian people from their homeland. We live in a world full of contradictions. Messages that confuse. Our moral compass shifts from black to white.

trees of home

Here I wait
Painting the trees of home
With their splendid, succulent,
splintered roots
Banana, Birch, Mango, Chilli,
Cherry,
Apple, Oak, Coconut, Palm, Plane
Here I paint
At the foot of the memory tree
Deep roots
Legs of skinny brown bark
holding up a blue world
My child is kissed
by a falling leaf
And kissed
And kissed
Here is the tree planted by my
grandfather on my daughter's
birthday

Now I sit in a London park
And paint and wait
To hold her in my arms
Among the saplings
The bright green leaves
The promise of spring
Sap-sweetness
Another summer
Now sparse winter,
bright red berries
Splintered
Season after season
I paint and wait
For these branches to bud.
To see my family again.

Refugees in collaboration with
Sita Brahmachari[8]

bycatch

There has been much publicity about the dangers of plastic to our marine life, and the poisoning of the world's oceans, but the biggest danger to our larger marine mammals and fish is fishing nets. The unintentional capture of whales, dolphins, porpoises, seals, turtles and sharks in a fishing haul is known as a bycatch.

Ghost nets, which are fishing nets left to drift in the open ocean, can also entangle a wide variety of marine life. It is a major welfare issue and causes a horrible death as the animals either starve or drown.

This problem has been around for decades and a lot of work is being done to try to balance marine conservation with the needs of the fishing industry.

Those in this industry need to consider how to have a lower impact on the marine life in their work. Even more important is workers allowing a shift in their perspective to become custodians of a wonderful resource so that generations of fishing will continue.

Most of us are not part of this industry, but the metaphor of the bycatch is helpful.

ROGER DODGER (FILM)

Roger Swanson: You can't sell a product without first making people feel bad.

Nick: Why not?

Roger Swanson: Because it's a substitution game. You have to remind them that they're missing something from their lives. Everyone's missing something, right?

Nick: I guess.

Roger Swanson: Trust me. And when they're feeling sufficiently incomplete, you convince them your product is the only thing that can fill the void. So instead of taking steps to deal with their lives, instead of working to root out the real reason for their misery, they go out and buy a stupid-looking pair of cargo pants.[9]

We can find ourselves entangled in a bycatch. For many it begins with the feeling we are missing out. On social media everyone portrays themselves at their best. Pictures of a fabulous place; eating an extraordinary meal; enjoying a wonderful relationship – a life in comparison to what we might think is our poverty-stricken one looks so much more inviting. We end up feeling inadequate, financially poor, emotionally poor, depressed and even suicidal.

A moment's exploration compelled by some advertising can turn without warning into something destructive, ultimately threatening the loss of our best selves. We find compulsions ruling us: to shop, to become famous, to gamble, to eat or not eat, to sext, all manner of fears, damaging relationships. These things will corral us and stop us living the life we had imagined for ourselves.

At times like this we need help. Wresting ourselves free from the entanglement of a sense of poverty through comparison is not easy. We were not designed to handle these things on our own. Alcoholics Anonymous' famous twelve steps to free alcoholics from addiction is remarkable, as it outlines a spiritual dynamic in the pursuit of healing. No one is expected to walk alone.

Change takes time, commitment, patience and ongoing consistency and motivation. The age-old 'people don't change' is a myth. It might be an attractive thought allowing the notions of 'I can't help the way I act. I can't be responsible. It's not my fault therefore I can't be punished.' Victor Hugo in his masterful book *Les Misérables* strove to answer the question 'Can a man change?' with a resounding 'yes'.

Investigating and discovering the help of God for ourselves and investing in healthy relationships are great ways forward. Finding friends is not easy and we certainly need to learn to be a friend as well as enjoy the fruit of friendship.

'I believe that we are here for each other, not against each other. Everything comes from an understanding that you are a gift in my life – whoever you are, whatever our differences.'

John Denver[10]

How to find a fresh perspective on our lives, to see what we have unintentionally allowed to entangle us? Never easy, often painful, not recommended to do alone, scary, but... we can't be brave if we're not scared. Be brave; freedom beckons.

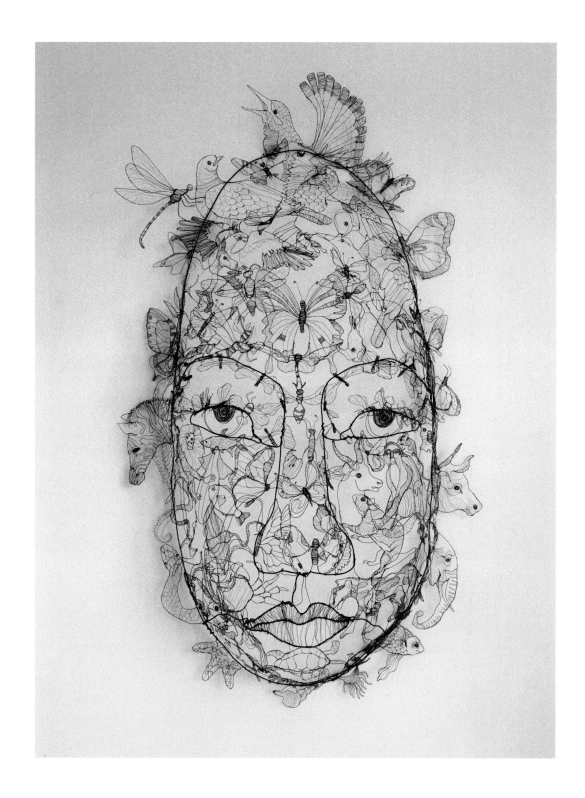

YOU ARE EVERYTHING
Fiona Morley / Stainless steel binding wire / W: 67 H: 114 D: 30cm

I belong to no particular religion, yet believe we are all part of something which could be named God. God is not separate from life. Through portraying the diversity of the animal kingdom in the face, I represent the consciousness and perception of our own lives, and interconnectedness with all other life – the closest explanation/experience of what God is.

TENDER ANGEL OF LIGHT

Mourl Ferryman / Encaustic painting / W: 61 H: 183cm

A portrait of my son, who has been both devil and angel to me and his brother. Our shared
faith and hope eventually brought him through his addiction. He now tenderly aids others
like himself towards self-awareness and love.

But what happens when we live God's way?

He brings gifts into our lives, much the same way that fruit appears in an orchard —

things like affection for others, exuberance about life, serenity.

We develop a willingness to stick with things,

a sense of compassion in the heart, and a conviction that a basic holiness permeates things and people.

We find ourselves involved in loyal commitments, not needing to force our way in life, able to marshal and direct our energies wisely.[11]

rest

These many mornings
I have woken,
opened my eyes,
seen the daylight once more
and thought of you.
Today I know I will awake in an
unimaginable, longed-for space,
and though I am ready,
my old heart beats fast in preparation
for its final slowing.

This bed I stir in,
I have stretched and yawned
to many new days,
wondering at their content.
Soft in my aloneness,
I remember the breath
of a long-gone warm body.
I leave those I love,
entrust their pain of loss,
the entirety of their living
to you
until...

My face is washed with earthy water
one more time
and I long for the sweetness
of your life-giving water –
soon to sip.

They offer fresh bedclothes, but
I will never need clothes again
for you will give me new.

Will I see a different sunrise
or moon-set?
Will I find my way?
Will my love be waiting?
Will we recognise each other?
Will I know what to do?

Call my name –
I will come and meet you,
we will walk in a new garden.

I hear the sound begin, the rising hum,
the song of goodness envelops me in
supernatural weightlessness.
The questions disappear;
I smile
as the meaning of 'rest'
reveals itself.

STAR TREK BEYOND[12]

Spock:
Fear of death
is illogical.

Bones:
Fear of death
is what keeps
us alive.

« Detail. See page 45

WHERE TRUTH IS, GOD IS

Matthew Hayward / Oil on canvas / W: 100 H: 70cm

This sombre depiction of women and children about to be murdered during the Holocaust
is a call for compassion and solidarity. Some of us see people of difference and need as
not fully human, which reminds us of the haunting words of Christ, that God is present in
those we deem to be the least of our brethren.

THE INNOCENT SUFFERER
Megan Leigh / Ink and watercolour / W: 18.5 H: 23.5cm

'I am poured out like water, and all my bones are out of joint. My heart has turned to wax; it has melted away within me' (Psalm 22:14, NIV 1984). This piece was born from the belief that God knows unimaginable suffering, and so I am not left alone in mine; that He was truly Godforsaken that I might never be.

GHOUTA, SYRIA

Bridget Adams / Hand-drawn, new media collage worked into using Karisma pencils / W: 123 H: 188cm

Ghouta is an area in south-western Syria that surrounds the city of Damascus. This image
depicts a scene of chaos and devastation as people are fleeing from a war zone. People
climb the ladders to safety and are rescued by empathy, respect and the goodness in us
all. Is this God?

LIGHT AND DARK

Natalie Maxted / Acrylic paint on canvas / W: 60 H: 60cm

A young boy sits; the light source on his side casts a shadow representing the darkness that follows him – an inevitable result of the light. This hopeful portrait symbolises the duality of God's light and the inescapable darkness in the human condition.

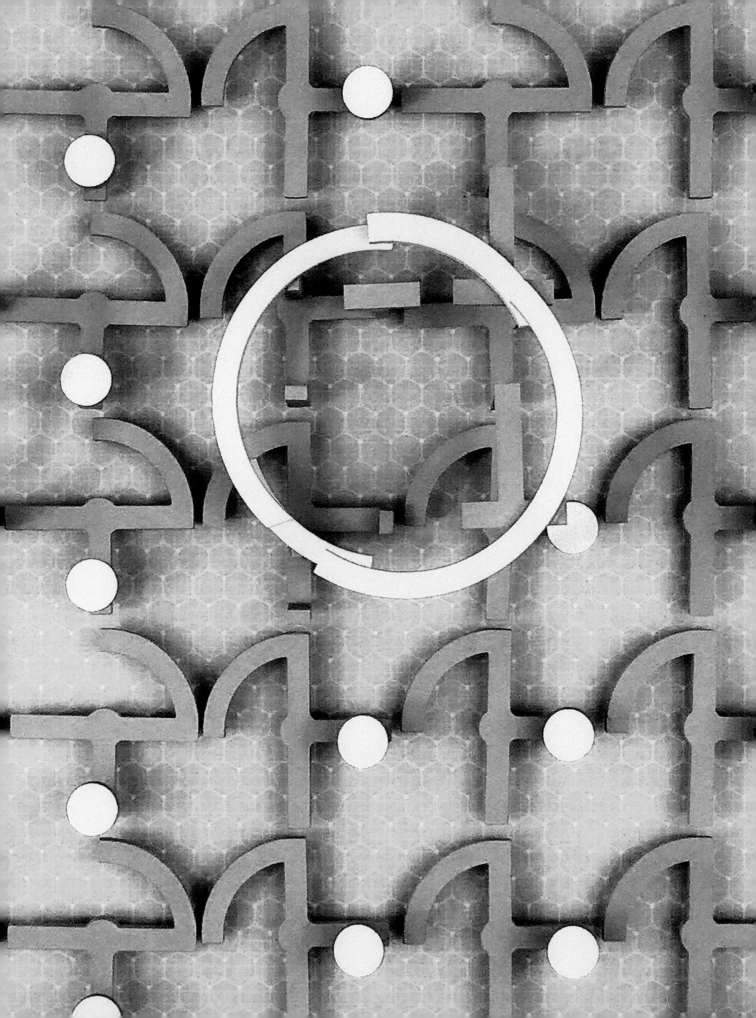

MURMURATION

The sound
of diverse
voices filled
with questions
rumbles over
the land like
the gathering
of an exquisite
murmuration
of starlings.
The threads
of God woven
into ordinary
everyday lives
are seen in so
many ways
– kindness,
respect for
others, our
visceral
responses to
nature and, oh,
so much more.
However many
find answers,
the questioning
sound will
never die.

ALL THAT IS SEEN AND UNSEEN
Marian Hall / Fabric, dye, Markal stik and thread / W: 46 H: 49cm

The overwhelming scale and beauty of the salt flats in the arid Atacama Desert inspired this piece. Large expanses of water fed by unseen underground reservoirs are found. The channel reminds us our world is complex and not always understood, but we know that God is the creator of all that is seen and unseen (Colossians 1:16).

symphony / part 1

What have we done?

The earth is laid waste.
It burns, it floods, it explodes,
it heaves in protest
and everything scatters.
Disaster follows disaster and the
stones of blame,
thrown by the wanton anonymous,
gouge, maim, tear down, destroy,
and responsibility
burns like incense
curling into the void.

Leaders line their pockets,
build expensive foxholes.
The land disintegrates,
and those with power to halt it
raise their glasses in their marbled
dwellings.
The people's lives are rubble-strewn,
they scratch for food,
reliant on the kindness of their fellows.
The goodness of the downtrodden
becomes the currency by which those in
power remain.

The ones who need give most
while others lined in comfort
stretch out their hands to take.
Hand-made gods of fame, money and
cynicism are honoured.
Secularism, the 'balanced' view,
the new exponent of belief.
Faith in Progress rises, its jackboots
trampling spirituality
into oblivion.

God is sated with the rising commotion
in service to the multi-gods of others.
An uproar that bloodies hands,
tears people apart,
deifies hatred, intolerance, violence
and purchases the mercy-less
rule of law,
trampling on the defenceless
and exploited.
Perfumed dogs rummaging in the dust
of death.

Can 'British values'[13] bring unity,
ignite common purpose?
See those money-laden criminals
who raze landscapes to the ground and
pay little,
who build exorbitant high-rise boxes.
Who are the faces of law incarcerated in
our prisons?
The poor, the people of colour, of
difference, of mental illness,
the abused, the broken, the neglected.
They gaze back through their bars –
mystified and abandoned.
Knowledge is placed beyond reach
of the dispossessed.
The once-fertile vines of council now
stripped, hacked, starved, desiccated,
and in the wake of famine the richness
of ordinary, everyday life
leaks away.
The homeless, the elderly,
the famine-stretched children,
the tortured middle classes,
cry for justice.

Why follow swaggering ability,
outstanding intelligence?
Why hope in pretentious ego?
Where are the honest judges and wise
counsellors?
Where is vision to thwart the perishing
of a people?
Remove fingers from ears,
strip blindfolds from eyes,
uncover shame.
Where is wisdom,
the fruit bowl of
understanding,
knowledge,
and hope,
to be found?

FORGIVENESS
Mia Pangilinan / Pencil on paper / W: 94 H: 70cm

God is benevolent. The Christian doctrine of the Trinity claims that God is one God, but also
three co-eternal persons: the Father, the Son (Jesus Christ) and the Holy Spirit. Here, God
is depicted as Jesus Christ in a modern interpretation of the crucifixion. An innocent Jesus
died for our sins, of which war is the greatest. His forgiveness is still available.

symphony / part 2

What story rules us?

Like a child ripped from its mother's
breast,
we have become a people plucked
from the deep-riven tracks of spirituality.
We have lost the map
to the ancient paths of
understanding,
peace, forgiveness, holiness
and family.

The inner informs the outer.
If we cannot find the landscape of
purpose,
how can we hope to walk in harmony
with each other?
Without a mutual spiritual sensitivity
beyond the absolute limitations of I, me
and mine,
foul becomes good and good is fouled,
and morality becomes relative.
We grab,
we lie,
we hate without restraint,
we cut, we maim,
we shore ourselves up with 'stuff',
view all with suspicion
because goodness became laughable.

Dying levels everything –
all we have will disintegrate.
Our grasping hands will empty.
Our money will devolve.
There will be nothing.
The coinage of our Time
revealed as spendthrift.

What if... God?
Is He?
What would He look like?
What could He do?
Does He care?
Does He listen?
Is He personal?
Can He change anything?
Can He rescue me and mine?

Underneath the surface of our society
are multifaceted strata,
threaded like gold in our culture
among the debris.
Look for them – watch and listen.
Prayers fill this nation.
Hope eddies into cracks of desolation.
Diversity bringing life,
weaving seeds of hope into our fabric –
new amid the stumps of the
ancient forest.

Search, search and search again,
dismiss distraction and focus,
cast off the shackles of determinism.
Look beyond the sight of the eye,
scoop the profound beauty of the divine
into ordinary life.
Let the trembling awe of otherness
prostrate us in humble worship
to hear again the harmonies of angelic
song and celebrate.

God is... God, and will remain forever
so, and we, His beloved creatures.

BRENDAN

Anne Smith / Quilt made from recycled fabrics, string and threads. / W: 76 H: 89cm

Artists are alert to glimpses of unvarnished reality which can become moments of revelation. I met homeless people weekly. They occupied little space in the world. I recycle clothes, so noticed the importance of their makeshift outfits. Brendan always wore a tie and stood up to shake my hand. In his politeness, trust, his gentle face and pure eyes, I saw the face of God.

Holiness

If God moved into my neighbourhood
I'd want to meet Him.
I'd have so many questions to which
there might be no answers.
Could I live with that?

If God became my neighbour
I'd want to watch everything He did.
I'd expect him to heal and help people.
Could I live with that?

If God walked into my house
I think I might collapse
because He'd know my name and
everything about me.
Could I live with that?

If God sat on the sofa beside me
I'd not move until He did
and never let my eyes or ears leave Him.
Could I live like that?

If God's Spirit decided to live inside me
I wouldn't be clean.
But He would
And I could live with that.

If God and I made home together
I would celebrate with everyone
because I'd know who I was
And I would live well with that.

What for?

How has it happened?

Values are fallen like pearls from a broken string and lie strewn on the floor. We hesitate to pick them up because of fear of the voices of derision. They are labelled as 'old-fashioned', replaced by baubles.

We do not know what to do with values because without 'Purpose' it's difficult to understand how things work once we put them together.

Science delves into the cause of all things and its findings fill us with wonder and often thankfulness. Yet science cannot answer the question of Purpose.

Imagine, as Lesslie Newbigin[14] would say, a clock. You discover this 'thing' but you have no idea whether to place it on a wall or throw it at a cat. Stripping the clock down to components and reassembling is possible. However, unless you knew what a clock was for, by talking either to the maker or to someone else who had learned its function, then the purpose would remain a mystery.

What if we human beings were created for a purpose?

What could that purpose be? Why is it important? Would it allow us to string values together?

Human beings carry the most amazing minds, with the capacity to think our way through everything our culture throws at us. For our own well-being and future hope, it is hugely important that we approach the stories that fill our lives with a healthy dose of scepticism. This is not the same as cynicism. There are many things that jump like hyped-up puppy dogs desperate for us to take them home. Refuse. If we took them all home, then they'd overtake our lives.

Rational thought impelled me to follow the God of the Bible who called me when I was nineteen years old. On investigation, living a life of love following someone I could learn to trust appeared a wonderful way to invest my short earthly life. A lifetime of learning will not be sufficient to know God, but my love and adoration of Him has only grown. His values became my values, His teaching the pathway of my life, which gained purpose, value and extraordinary richness.

HUMANITAS

John Afflick / Oil, distemper, gold and copper leaf and pastiglio on a traditional gesso panel / W: 67.5 H: 97cm

A personification of the virtue 'Kindness', one of seven virtues, represented by the ladders needed to reach an understanding of what God is... Is a full understanding of what God is possible if we fall short of his glory (see Romans 3:23), slip on the rungs and repeatedly slide down the backs of ancient serpents? No! I am, you are, and GOD IS what GOD IS.

THE VOICE OF NATURE

Zeinab Harding / Limewood / W: 58 H: 140 D: 6cm

Carved in limewood and inspired by the sacred walls of the Altar of Peace in Rome, my
work weaves together the ancient use of floral ornament to symbolise the divine and my
own experience of seeing and hearing God through nature.

'Where is the Life
we have lost in
living?

Where is the
wisdom we have
lost in knowledge?

Where is the
knowledge we have
lost in information?'

T S Eliot[15]

wisdom

I n the twilight, a murmuration of starlings moves as angel wings over the land. The unfathomable beauty of 100,000 birds in harmonious flight lifts our eyes to the evening sky in wonder.

A fear of death murmurs over the UK and many other countries in the world, its darkness locking us away from each other. The announcement of mass vaccination in December 2020 became the ray of hope that lifted spirits at the end of a tough year. Scientists have managed the unimaginable and within less than twelve months have engineered several effective vaccines.

It is a vast enterprise to inoculate any nation, and caution continues to advocate the use of masks, social distancing, social bubbles and adhering to each country's restrictions. The discovery of several additional strains of exceptionally virulent COVID has led to lockdown again for the UK and others, in the race against time for the delivery of the vaccine.

Confronted with catastrophic scenarios, the decision-making of most governments struggled, and many people bawl for wise leaders able to make positive decisions in the face of a capricious storm.

Facing the inevitability of death rather than succumbing to the fear of it is one pillar of wisdom. It brings perspective to the question: what is important in life? The desire to have spent more hours at work are not the last words of a dying person.

It's easy to confuse knowledge with wisdom. Wisdom is full of humanity and humility. Wisdom listens, takes time to understand and puts itself in the shoes of someone with whom it disagrees. It doesn't shout its view, but commits itself to peace, revealing the qualities of peacemaker, its presence a refreshing relief. It has learnt to live with uncertainty and knows 'rightness' is a balance, because wisdom will not stop its quest to learn. It studies the past, but wisdom never makes the mistake of living there. Brimming with curiosity, it looks forward with hope to a positive future. Where to find wisdom? Search it out…

[My father] would sit me down and drill me:

'Take this to heart.
Do what I tell you – live!

Sell everything and buy Wisdom!
Forage for Understanding!

Don't forget one word! Don't deviate an inch!

Never walk away from Wisdom – she guards your life;

love her – she keeps her eye on you.

Above all and before all, do this: Get Wisdom!

Write this at the top of your list: Get Understanding!

Throw your arms around her – believe me, you won't regret it;

never let her go – she'll make your life glorious.

She'll garland your life with grace,

she'll festoon your days with beauty.' [16]

murmuration

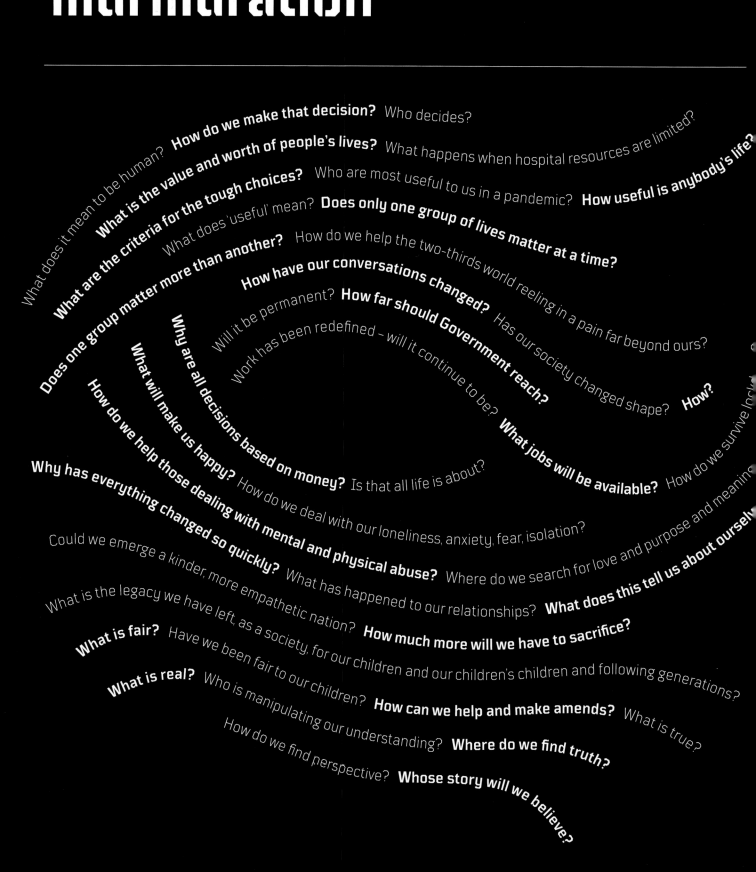

How do we make that decision? Who decides?

What does it mean to be human? What is the value and worth of people's lives? What happens when hospital resources are limited?

What are the criteria for the tough choices? Who are most useful to us in a pandemic? How useful is anybody's life?

What does 'useful' mean? Does only one group of lives matter at a time?

Does one group matter more than another? How do we help the two-thirds world reeling in a pain far beyond ours?

How have our conversations changed? Has our society changed shape? How?

Will it be permanent? How far should Government reach?

Work has been redefined – will it continue to be? What jobs will be available? How do we survive lock

Why are all decisions based on money? Is that all life is about?

What will make us happy? How do we deal with our loneliness, anxiety, fear, isolation?

How do we help those dealing with mental and physical abuse? Where do we search for love and purpose and meaning

Why has everything changed so quickly? What has happened to our relationships? What does this tell us about ourselv

Could we emerge a kinder, more empathetic nation? How much more will we have to sacrifice?

What is the legacy we have left, as a society, for our children and our children's children and following generations?

What is fair? Have we been fair to our children?

What is real? Who is manipulating our understanding? How can we help and make amends? What is true?

Where do we find truth?

How do we find perspective? Whose story will we believe?

HORIZON

Xander Haywood / Oil on canvas / W: 100 H: 120cm

'Horizon' encapsulates what God means to me; God is nature with its infinite fractal and interconnected forms. God is felt when I gaze deeply into the vast sky. The experience of losing the sense of a separate self and dissolving into the landscape as just a point of awareness.

TRILOGY
Karl Newman / Oil on canvas / W: 140 H: 118cm

The painting was inspired by the idea that God is community, three persons in one, a team, a family, which includes us. It is also loosely based on a homecoming, the story of the return of the prodigal son.

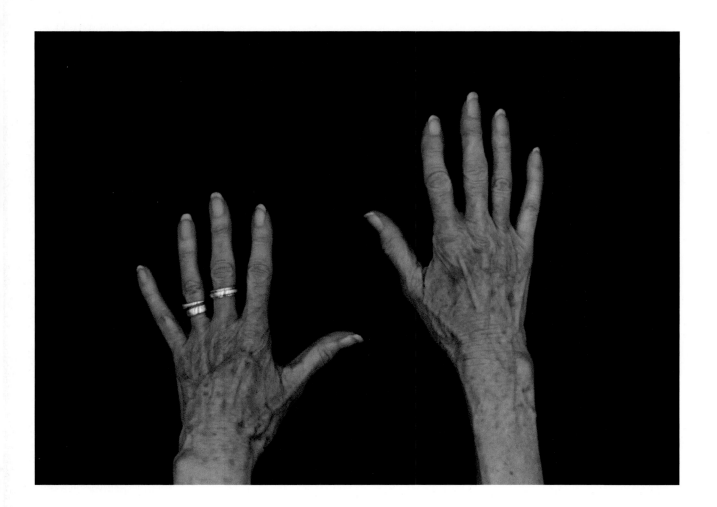

HANDS (FILM)
Andy Hunter / Film and music / Length: 3.33min

God is our hands. We ask God to intervene in the world around us as if expecting some miracle, but we forget that on the end of our arms are God's hands. Hands for doing, helping, giving, extending the hand of friendship. Society would be a much better place if we realised this.

NO BODY (FILM)

Haemin Ko / A film with whole frame-by-frame charcoal drawings twenty five frames per second / Length: 4.33 min

'No Body' is an autobiographical, poetic, experimental hand-drawn short animation film. The story is giving thoughts of the city and me through three emotional chapters of excitement/frustration/hope based on the last ten years of artist immigration experience in London.

UNCERTAINTY

In an uncertain world, deciding which story to believe and follow is a seminal decision. It is important to many that their personal commitments are witnessed by others, asking family and friends to help by calling them to account on their vows. In many cultures water plays an important part – to cleanse from uncleanness, which some call 'sin', together with an anticipation to live a changed way of life. The action carries themes of death and mortality with the expectation of rebirth, allowing the light of God to illuminate the heart with wisdom and guidance.

celebrate

Feet become feathers,
elevate and swirl,
flip-flop without fear,
float without tether.

Eyes
woken from sleep,
unearth beauty... everywhere.
Faces uncloak
and rivulets of joy
corkscrew through
unguarded bodies.

Unexpected delight
gurgles from depths,
geysers of happiness
erupt
sprinkling others
with unbounded delight.

Arms reach
to the sky.
Music tracks
the breathless life.
Uninhibited praise
bursts –
its fireworks
bathing the air
with gold.

an ordinary life

desire to live an ordinary life. This is not a fashionable aspiration. I live in a culture where people aim to be extraordinary. Perhaps through making huge amounts of money. Growing a business, the name of which rests on the tip of everybody's tongue. To be 'famous' or 'infamous', or to be known and remembered by demonstrating a unique virtue or ability. A hope to make an indelible mark on this planet that will exist long after our death.

The goal of an ordinary life is not this.

The goal of an ordinary life is undervalued.

What might it look like?

It is making home wherever we find ourselves so that returning is a joy. A place where we can be who we are, let go of everything in the day that threatens to overwhelm. It is our place of rest and recuperation. It usually involves sharing the space with others – family, friends, lover.

This should be a space where there are no toxic relationships, but mutually rewarding ones. If we do find ourselves in a toxic relationship, then let's be brave and seek help to restore our equilibrium. We all need help at times. Positive relationships are difficult, demanding, but, oh, so rewarding. Family relationships require careful thought and awareness. This includes the ability to forget the slights and arguments, to be the adult when everyone around appears to be turning into a toddler, to hold on, hold through and redeem the undoubted rewards.

To notice the everyday life takes time, care and attention to detail. To live it

beautifully means we have learned to find joy in the everyday, worked to cultivate a heart of thankfulness and gratitude and, above all, understood something of what it means to love. A positive outlook that aims to find purpose in the new day, enjoying the good things, letting go of the unhelpful. Crazy, difficult things happen and we all get wounded and grief-stricken. That's when we need the people who care about us the most.

There is a practical need to get on top of our income and outgoings, eat as healthily as we can, and learn to be a friend. Three areas most of us need help with. We all want and need friends, but waiting around for it to happen will be disappointing. Generating positive things inside ourselves to give to others is a constructive way forward. To view each other and ourselves with kindness and generosity. Being a friend requires availability, often at the wrong time for us. It might be that our own life is unravelling, but one of the best ways to stop its collapse is to care for someone else. We might end up feeling we always do the inviting and no one ever invites us back. What we give does come back to us – in unexpected ways.

Self-centredness and the clinging to our 'rights' can at times know no bounds, but is destructive. At heart we want connection – a sense of belonging and being loved. Whoever we are, however much our life is adorned with 'things', we are all in search of love. Learning to love well is one of the hardest things we will ever do.

The unlooked-for fruit in an attitude of giving ourselves away to others is that we change. Things begin to happen in our lives that are unforeseen, heartening and delightful. We start to realise we are no longer alone, that we have 'backup'.

'Suddenly I realised – two people isn't enough. You need backup. If you're only two people, and someone drops off the edge, then you're on your own. Two isn't a large enough number. You need three at least.'[17]

There is one question that will help us think through what kind of life we want:

What would we like to be remembered for when we die?

An honest answer to that question can be transformational, because the second question is:

What are we doing to achieve it?

A CROWN OF THORNS
Jane Morgan / Bronze (selenium and copper) patinated / W: 17.5 H: 5. D: 18.5cm Weight: 1kg

This work considers the familiar visual image of a crown of thorns: one of the most emotive and identifiable iconographies in religious art. A supreme symbol posing questions and invoking intellectual interpretation. The crown's simple natural form starkly juxtaposes the complex immediate visual elements, eliciting both meaning and physical identity.

GOD HEALS

Anila Hussain / Metallic black and white print on Fujifilm paper with frame / W: 50 H: 50cm

A gritty metallic print of the hands of an elderly woman, praying; she is riddled with long-term pain and turns to her faith for God to heal her and give her comfort. She talks to God five times a day, praying one day she will wake up and she will be healed.

'We sail within
a vast sphere,
ever drifting in
uncertainty,
driven from end
to end.'

Blaise Pascal[18]

ghosts

More –
more certainty,
more stability,
more understanding,
more meaning.
We are fragile,
pushed, pressed,
tugged by alternatives.
Inside we are alone.

Turbulent times
uncover nakedness,
expose emptiness.
Bones and heart ache.
The artificial
hollows us out.

The ghosts of transcendence
haunt.
The sense of
more
beckons.

'I caught the Holy Spirit in the basement of my mind and flung him out of there ... Atheism is a long and cruel business. I believe I've been through it to the end. For the last years I've been like a man who no longer has any reason to live.'

Jean-Paul Sartre[19]

GOD IS NOT A POLEMICIST

Wayne Clough / Oil paint on gesso board / W: 30.5 H: 40cm

This is a painting of the philosopher and activist Bertrand Russell. Russell described himself as both an agnostic and an atheist. While his opinions regarding religion were polemical, he was, however, a pacifist and through direct action sought to oppose war in all its guises.

CLEANSED

Matthew Hayward / Oil on canvas / W: 100 H: 100cm

Hindu worshippers in the process of ritual bathing as communion with their gods. It is as if spiritual power is imbibed from the water and the ritual washes away sin as well as reinforcing a sense of community.

BAPTISM

Gabrielle-Aimée Séguin / Oil, acrylic and acrylic spray paint on canvas / W: 64 H: 90cm

A portrait of my ten-year-old sister, painted to celebrate her baptism and exhibited during the ceremony in early October at Old Windsor Parish Church. I wanted to depict the meaning of this religious initiation as a spiritual experience removed from the physical world.

THE LIGHT

Teakster / Mixed media on Kodak Metallic / W: 42 H: 59.4cm

In the Islamic faith, the Light is one of the ninety-nine beautiful names of God. God is the divine light of all the worlds, whose light illuminates the heart; the One who is the light of wisdom and guidance, making the obscure clear by clearing away darkness.

REFLECTION

Jake Flood / Photograph / W: 45 H: 30cm

The Font, Gloucester Cathedral. The reflections edging the font mirror the ancient stories expressed in the surrounding stained glass. The centre is empty, offering a space to reflect and connect with God. I don't believe in any deity, but working with survivors of slavery, moments of reflection, silence and stillness have expanded to enable community, cooperation and the beginnings of new stories – maybe that is God.

APO ANNO

Jake Tiongan de los Reyes / Planks of wood and plaster, acrylic and ink / W: 70 H: 70cm

'Apo Anno' is a prime representation of the Igorots – an indigenous tribe in the cordillera of northern Philippines. It depicts our identity and heritage. We believe Kabunyan (God) is the focal point of our existence. We cling to this as it is the only truth we come to know. This gift of a lifetime from our forefathers, containing a message of goodwill, is given to every child.

ADMISSION
Patrick Morales-Lee / Pencil, acrylic paint and charcoal powder / W: 63.5 H: 89cm

This work is inspired by the ceremony of baptism – the idea of taking on something new, of transformation, that people will participate physically and mentally in an action to show to themselves, to show to others, that they believe, that there is meaning in the process.

THRESHOLD

Where to find the signs of God in our world? There are many places. For some it is found in the silence. For others, the natural world. For Moses, in the biblical story, it was a non-burning burning bush that caught his attention. What will capture ours? Our preparation for an encounter is perhaps shedding artifice and protection, and preparing ourselves for an intimate and direct conversation.

If God is real, we can expect Him to reveal Himself.

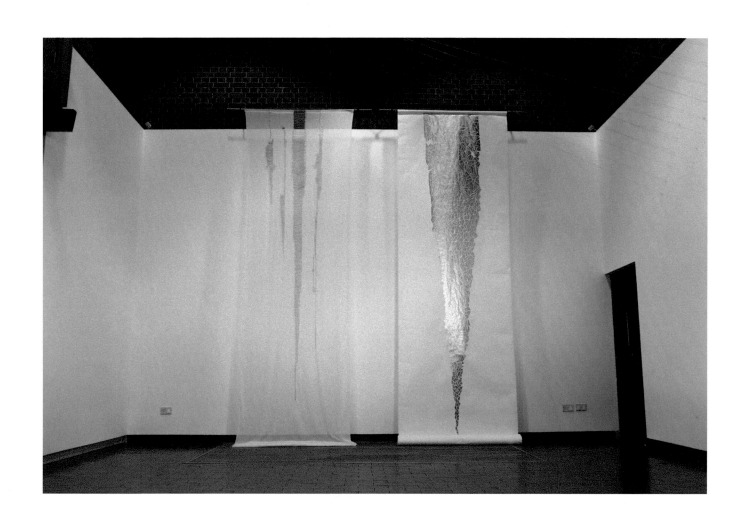

SHARDS AND SEAMS

Kirsty Kerr / Installation (materials: paper, fabric, thread) / W: 150 H: 400 D: 40cm

A reflection on the journey from brokenness to restoration. The work references the Japanese technique of kintsugi (embracing flaws and imperfections in broken pottery by mending into wholeness with seams of gold). God is... partnering with us in our frailty and re-creating our world from the broken and discarded parts that remain. A re-creative beauty that lingers dormant in the most discarded and unwanted people.

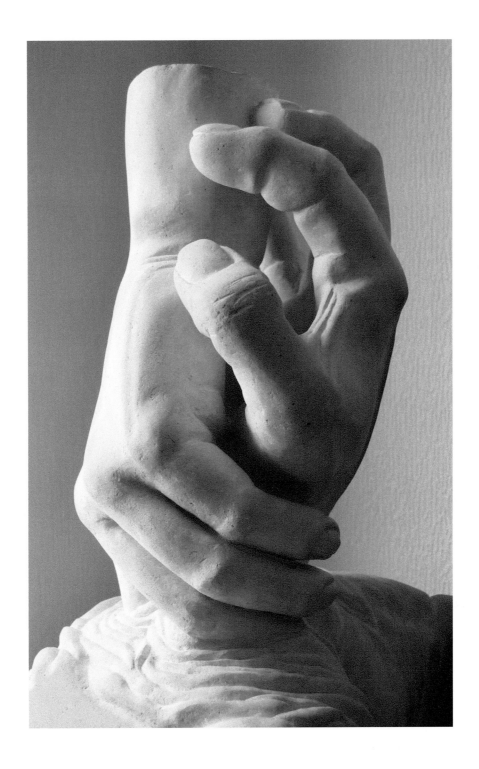

GOD IS RESCUER: CONNECTION

Deborah Harrison / Portland Stone / W: 35 H: 70 D: 35cm Weight: 250kg

A carving in Portland Stone. One hand is reaching down to grasp another drowning hand. It is based on the testimony of an ex-addict in Gloucester. It links to the story of Jesus pulling Peter out of the sea. Carved when a news article showed the drowned child of an asylum seeker.

rewilding

The city is a world of constant noise. While some of it is loud – footings dug for a new building – other sounds create the background hum a city-dweller hardly notices. The rumbling sound of traffic interrupted by an emergency service vehicle; the sound of a plane in take-off or landing; a police helicopter circling. Road crossings, bunches of people waiting to traverse, the beeping signal beckoning buggies, people, dogs, the odd streetwise cat. The sound of people on the city street walking, chatting, running, dealing with a small child's crisis, doors opening and closing, bells, horns. Many of us extricate ourselves using earphones to access the sound of our choice – a podcast, music, programme, presenter. Adverts shove images at us on walls, buses, cars, taxis. This human world craves our attention. Noise that fills us up and leaves no space for reflection.

Where to go to shut out all distractions? How to zero in to go beyond ourselves? How to go away in order to return?

For many of us, the natural world is a potent way to divest ourselves of the garment of everyday life and 'rewild' our being. By this I mean finding a space where the stuff of everyday life can be dropped. Where thoughts that prickle, distract, undermine, crowd like an unwieldy flock of crows, can be quieted. Thus released, with empty hands, the opportunity to think and contemplate,

learn, gain fresh perspective and renew our strength is possible. A deliberate act of exorcising ourselves from the domination of our environment as a way of purposeful exposure to the spiritual.

Nourishment comes from picking, eating, chewing, swallowing and digesting, and takes time. We are about the potent business of waking part of ourselves that is normally shut down. Allowing ourselves to become myopic and focus on the tiny in order to find a way into the hugeness of the universe.

Senses heighten, previously unheard tiny sounds begin to magnify, unexpected moments astonish, magical connections establish and then unbidden tears may flow.

And yet we do not need to leave the city in order to focus myopically on some element that will uncover the world of the divine. We can work in concert with our habitat, pressing in to cultivate and water it, discovering the presence of God within it.

Perhaps with work we will discover that God is found precisely where we find ourselves.

'I want to be cured.

Of a craving for something I cannot find

And of the shame of never finding it.'

T S Eliot[20]

« Detail. See page 86

IN THE SILENCE

Ashar / Oil on wooden panel / W: 100 H: 100cm

In response to the question, God is…, this piece is about silence; taking time to still the mind. Allowing access to source and the elation silence brings – all will be found there; within. Listen. 'Silence is the language of God, all else is poor translation' (Rumi).

ADMITTING THE POSSIBILITIES OF ERROR: GOD IS...? THE PUZZLE

Kirsten Lavers / Mixed media – plywood, pyrography and gold / 42cm diameter circle

'Think it possible that you may be mistaken.' Advices & Queries #17 *Quaker Faith And Practice*. A puzzle of a drawing which includes whimsy pieces symbolic of ways humankind has answered questions about God. One place God (or Good) might be found in our twenty-first-century world is in the process of learning from, and acceptance of, our mistakes as well as those made by others.

EROSION: GOD IS BETRAYED

Wendy Campbell-Briggs / Sculptural ceramic art / W: 70 H: 100cm Weight: 3kg

Genesis 1:26-31, God creates humans and gives them the Earth to care for... Pebbles are progressively worn smooth by the relentless motion of the sea. We are responsible for rising sea levels which speed up the erosion of our coastline – the ceramic vessels in my work capture the very essence of our world under stress, and the fragility of our environment.

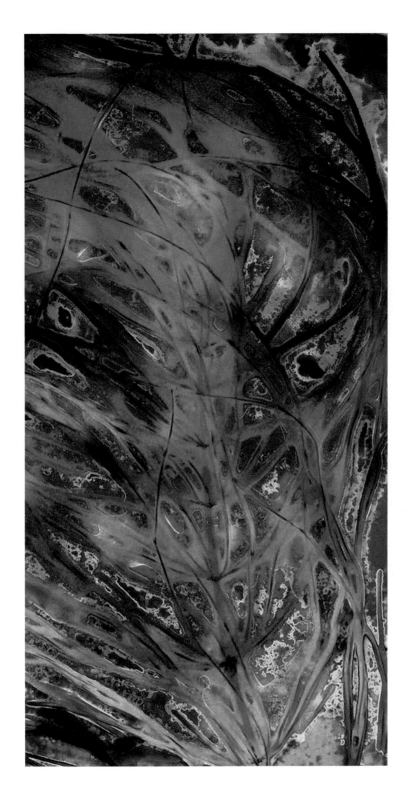

GOD IS I AM

Claire Griffiths / Digitised lumen cyanotype mounted on a commercial LED panel / W: 60 H: 120cm

In the biblical account of Moses, God attracts his attention through a flaming bush. God reveals His name as I AM, placing Himself forever present with and outside of time. The vibrant energy and charge reflected in this image alludes to this biblical account. How does God get our attention in our time and place?

be

Stillness
Where, how?
The endless
nibbling of life
The stress of
merciless doing

The quietude of
emptying
The fear of
nothingness
Unfilled hands held
in supplication
The overwhelming
need for filling

Be
Exhale
Breathe
Release
Wait
Listen

transfusion

I believe another,
not him.
A cup of bitterness taints my being.
My eyes fail me,
I lose the light
and my life disengages
and halts.

Movement spied in my darkness
frightens then brings relief.
I am not dying alone,
but dying we are.
The battering storm of hope denied
will abandon us to Fate.

A flicker flecks my blindness.
I fall prostrate
as flecks materialise into Him,
my true and tender Father.

Held in His unbreakable arms
I still …
The storm may do its worst,
slathered in His salve of love,
hope's transfusion
gently renews my being.
Do not fear the pain –
it sings the song of life.

'The world is too much with us; late and soon,

Getting and spending, we lay waste our powers; –

Little we see in Nature that is ours.'

William Wordsworth[21]

CONVERSATION

Judy Clarkson / Oil on canvas / W: 150 H: 100cm

God is... within and without: a conversation between the individual and the infinite. The figure and the landscape are timeless. The dark water represents a spiritual world with the capacity to encompass us all. The man is naked, without protection or artifice: his relationship with God intimate and direct.

'Our lifelong nostalgia, our longing to be reunited with something in the universe from which we now feel cut off, to be on the inside of some door which we have always seen from the outside, is no mere neurotic fancy, but the truest index of our real situation. And to be at last summoned inside would be both glory and honour beyond all our merits and also the healing of that old ache.'

CS Lewis[22]

'Tis madness – yet how often we, to gain the fruit, cut down the tree.'

The Satires of Cynicus[23]

God Is...

In Genesis in the Bible we read the story of Adam and Eve and a serpent that can speak. This serpent is bent on deception. He speaks to Eve, not for her good, but to undermine the relationship she has with her Creator. This Creator has generated a whole earth to be explored, tilled and filled by both her and Adam. The serpent casts doubt on the trustworthiness of God by questioning the one thing that God had commanded. Of one tree He forbade Adam and her to eat – the tree of the knowledge of good and evil. Eating of its fruit meant they would die.

The serpent insinuated God was lying and in eating they would not die. Also, by rebelling against this command they would receive even more than God had promised and would become like Him.

The seeds of doubt, of self-interest, of self-aggrandisement, rebellion and becoming like God lay in the fruit's eating. Eve, on studying it, could not resist and she ate. It tasted so good she offered it to Adam, who also ate. In that moment they brought upon themselves the incalculable tragedy of separation from their Maker and the one inescapable part of life as we know it – death.

Inherent in this story is how a simple, outwardly harmless action – as innocuous as eating a piece of fruit – can have immeasurable repercussions.

How often have we listened to the insinuating, destructive voice within? We choose to eat the wrong fruit without thinking through the ramifications of the pain and turmoil that will follow. In the fallout of that choice, we remember the longing to rescind the moment, and make a different decision. But there is no going back.

In the Bible story, Adam and Eve are thrown out of Eden and God blocks their return by an angel holding a flaming sword. We cannot go back and undo what we have done, no matter how contrite, upset or ashamed of ourselves we are. In our fatal choice, we aligned ourselves with a flawed world that exhibits a deep capacity for cruelty and unfairness, where neighbour kills neighbour.

Yet deep within is a suspicion that life could be different. There grows a longing for everything rich in joy: relationships, children – ours or other people's – family, community. To work together to care for each other and our world, to live a different, contributory life. We sense there is a voice of goodness alongside the lying voice of destruction. We feel the need to search for different fruit that brings positive things like 'love, joy, peace, patience, kindness, goodness, faithfulness, gentleness and self-control'.[24] The kind of life that allows thankfulness and gratitude for what we have and the world in which we live. A world filled with beauty and wonder despite us.

Our challenge is to work against the voice that lies. To choose to spurn self-absorption and learn altruism. To eat from the fruit that allows our thoughts and actions to exhibit our best selves.

It is but a prayer away.

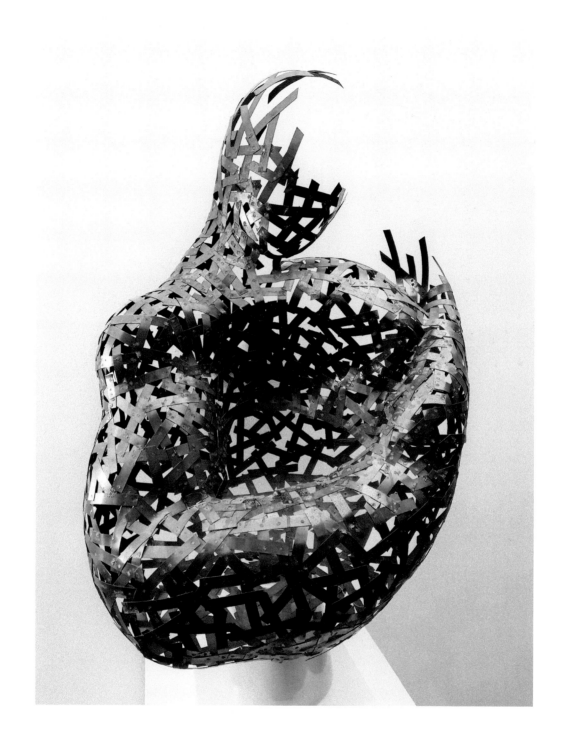

BEING

Sarah E Choi / A spot-welding metal sculpture / W: 55 H: 84 D: 43cm Weight: 3.5kg

In my diverse, multicultural society, love, comfort, joy, loneliness and tragedy are all interspersed with a clear message of my concern and hope for humanity. Each sharp metal strip represents a moment of our up-and-down lives. The smooth whole expresses the hope we have in Christ that makes us journey on... God is with us always!

SOUL WITHIN

Teresa Chlapowski / Sand cast glass, copper inclusions, on a ceramic base / W: 16 H: 47 D:5cm Weight: 6kg

God is within us but also all around us. This piece aims to bring together all the different layers that make us who we are: a part of God. We are beings on different levels, made of the stars but harbouring a spirituality not of this physical world.

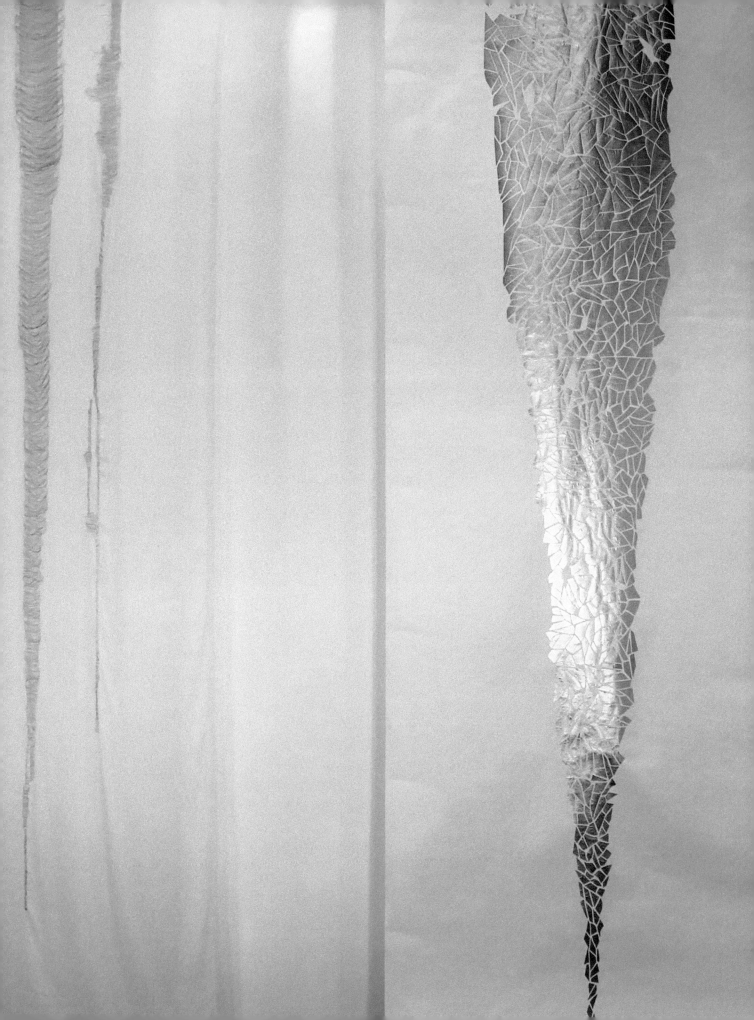

light

Night abates
aerated with painterly orange.
The crescent moon,
strongest at its ebbing,
tugs the rising curtain
of unfolding daybreak.

A robin flies.
In wide-eyed civil dawn
fooled, it slaps into glass
and falls, stunned.
Sure-footed still it lands
until with shrug and speckle
swifts into the bird-song sky.

The veiled light separates cloud
from sea.
The artist's fiery red
dyes the sea-hanging, earth-hovering,
soft-bellied cloud
gliding sonorously above
coal-black water.

The world turns,
bowing to the hidden blood-red bard,
its unusual modesty
touching the expansive sky
with vermillion brilliance.

Wondrous light.
Glorious effulgence.
Made for earth's
sweet cycles
becomes a daily votive offering
of inventive praise.

Sublime Creator,
what greatness of thought,
largess of sight,
wisdom of sequence,
detail of nourishment,
ageless rhythm,
incandescent beauty,
voicing life in all its fullness,
that all may feast
and thrive.

EXHIBITION

Lesley Sutton, Curator for Chaiya Art Awards at gallery@oxo, Oxo Tower Wharf

The invitation to explore the question 'God is…' was met by an overwhelming response of varied visual stories, emotions and philosophies from more than 700 artists across the country. It is a part of the human condition to question our existence; to wonder, to imagine and to try to make sense of the world we inhabit, how we came to be here and what will happen to us when we die.

Art enables us to think and question not just with our minds, but also through our bodies, our senses. The tacit nature of cold marble mimicking the vulnerability and warmth of flesh, the fragility of fine porcelain candlelit shelters reminding us of the ease with which our places of safety can be broken through war, debt, grief or broken relationships. As viewers, our eyes meet the emotions of the artists, their colour palettes revealing personal narratives. Some speak of pain and suffering, questioning where God is when days are dark and He seems to have abandoned us. Others have used brightly coloured canvases of cerulean blue, gilded squares or intricately carved sculptures to invite us to delight in the beauty of the world we call home. Yet others have chosen to remind us of our responsibility as caretakers of the earth and sea and all its inhabitants.

It has been a difficult but joyful task to be part of selecting and curating the artworks in this book from so many interesting works and to share the underlying common threads that lay beneath the majority of the creative responses submitted. I hope that you will see something of your own story in this book; the pain, the beauty and the joy that are a part of our human condition, no matter what our story is.

So, look, listen, engage and share your story with us, and allow yourself to be surprised by what you receive as you make your own response to the question, God is…

Lesley Sutton

Lesley Sutton is a curator and fibre-based artist from Manchester. She is the founding director of PassionArt, a charity that explores the way art and faith impact our everyday lives.

Our Charity partner Unseen works to end human trafficking and modern slavery.

Unseen works across the UK with government and key agencies, as well as directly with survivors; runs the UK Modern Slavery Helpline; provides emergency safehouse accommodation; supports survivors in recovering from their trauma and living in freedom and safety in the community.

Unseen also uses art as therapy to aid recovery of survivors.

Chaiya Art Awards helps fund this vital work by donating a percentage of all artwork sold from the 2021 exhibition at the gallery@oxo.

UNSEEN: Registered charity no. 1127620

THE ART OF HEALING

At Unseen, we often see the value and benefit of therapeutic art and craft activities for the people we support. Whether it is with residents in our Safehouses or with groups of survivors rebuilding their lives in the community, we know that when survivors take part in creative activities it gives them the opportunity to explore their feelings in imaginative and reflective ways.

Our partnership with the Chaiya Art Awards celebrates and supports the therapeutic value of creativity and the deeply important role that it can play in the process of healing.

'A relationship with our imagination is a relationship with our deepest self.' Connection with the imagination can be a transformational step in a person's healing. It helps survivors to process their past and, importantly, to develop the courage to begin imagining a safe and more positive future.

Kate Garbers, Co-Founder and Director, Unseen UK

> 'A relationship with our imagination is a relationship with our deepest self.'
>
> **Pat B Allen**[25]

www.unseenuk.org

ACKNOWLEDGEMENTS

Book text written by:
Ann Clifford

Art compiled by:
Lesley Sutton, Ann Clifford, Katrina Moss

Judges:
Marcus Lyon, Clive Davis, Jonathan Evens,
Deborah Tompsett, Katrina Moss

Exhibition curators:
Lesley Sutton, Mike Thorpe

Exhibition installer:
Scott Miles

Marketing and PR:
Helen Farquharson, Katie Carter, Kate Burke

Book design:
David Salmon

Website and graphic design:
Micah Purnell

Sponsors:
The Jerusalem Trust
Westhill Trust
Souter Charitable Trust

With thanks from Ann

To Instant Apostle, our publishers, and David our designer, all of whom are wonderful to work with.

To Katrina, my dear friend, with whom I have great big adventures.

To my husband, Steve, who loves surprises and adventures as much as I do.

To West London Writers, the group who have taught me so much.

To the God whom I follow and never quite know where I will end up next.

With thanks from Katrina

To all the artists who entered the awards, sharing with us your creativity, imagination and skills. We thoroughly enjoyed seeing your artwork and it is such a shame that we can only display a fraction of the wonderful work submitted.

To everyone who has had any input into the Chaiya Art Awards, your contribution large or small is so, so appreciated.

To the one who sustains and encourages me – I cannot truly express my thanks:

God, you have my heart.

CITATIONS

1. **Cited in Matthew Richard Schlimm,** *This Strange and Sacred Scripture* (Baker Academic, 2015), p.27 . . . . Page 02

2. **Curator of Viva Arte Viva,** 57th Venice Biennale 2017, www.labiennale.org/en/art/2017/introduction-christine-macel . . Page 05

3. **James Baldwin,** '*Confronting History: James Baldwin*', Kinfolk,
https://www.kinfolk.com/confronting-history-james-baldwin/ . . . . Page 12

4. **Nelson Mandela,** *Long Walk to Freedom* (Little, Brown and Company, 1994) . . . . Page 13

5. **Stephen Fry,** cited in '*Being Human: The problem is me*', Evangelical Alliance,
https://www.eauk.org/what-we-do/initiatives/being-human/season-2/episode-3. . . . . Page 13

6. **Peter Lynas and Jo Frost,** '*Being Human*', IDEA magazine Jan/Feb 2020 . . . . Page 17

7. **Source:** UN High Commission for Refugees, https://www.unhcr.org/figures-at-a-glance.html . . . . Page 35

8. **From the art and writing class at Islington Centre for Refugees and Migrants run by Sita Brahmachari
and artist-in-residence Jane Ray,** www.amnesty.org.uk/blogs/stories-rights/poetry-portal-togetherness.
Used by permission . . . . Page 38

9. *Roger Dodger* (directed by Dylan Kidd, 2002) . . . . Page 39

10. **John Denver,** 1943–97, an American singer-songwriter, record producer, actor, activist and humanitarian.
www.brainyquote.com/quotes/john_denver_187921/ (accessed 4th February 2020) . . . . Page 39

11. **Galatians 5:22-24,** *The Message.* . . . . Page 42

12. *Star Trek Beyond* (directed by Justin Lin, 2016) Distributed by Paramount Pictures . . . . Page 43

13. **According to Ofsted directly from the Government,** 'Fundamental British Values' to be taught in schools
comprise: 'democracy', 'the rule of law', 'individual liberty', 'mutual respect for and tolerance of those
of different faiths and beliefs, and those without faith.' www.youngcitizens.org/british-values
(accessed 5th February 2020) . . . . Page 51

14. **Bishop Lesslie Newbigin,** 1909-98, theologian, missioligist, missionary and author. . . . . Page 55

15. **www.brainyquote.com/quotes/t_s_eliot_121647** (accessed 21st February 2020) . . . . Page 58

16. **Proverbs 4:3b-9,** *The Message.* . . . . Page 59

17. *About a Boy* (directed by Chris Weitz and Paul Weitz, 2002) Distributed by Universal Pictures . . . . Page 67

18. **Blaise Pascal,** 1623–62, French mathematician, physicist, inventor, writer and Catholic theologian . . . . Page 70

19. **Jean-Paul Sartre, 'The Words'.** Translated from the French by Bernard Frechtman (New York: George Braziller
Inc, 1964), cited in Charlie Cleverly, *The Discipline of Intimacy* (Colorado Springs, CO: David C Cook, 2019) . . . . Page 71

20. **T S Eliot,** *The Cocktail Party* (1949) . . . . Page 83

21. **William Wordsworth,** 'The World Is Too Much With Us',
www.poetryfoundation.org/poems/45564/the-world-is-too-much-with-us (accessed 24th February 2020) . . . . Page 89

22. **CS Lewis,** *The Weight of Glory,* © copyright CS Lewis Pte Ltd 1949. . . . . Page 91

23. **Martin Anderson,** 1854–1932 (better known by his pseudonym Cynicus), *The Satires of Cynicus.*
Scottish artist, political cartoonist, postcard illustrator and publisher . . . . Page 92

24. **Galations 5:22-23,** NIV, 1984. . . . . Page 93

25. **Pat B Allen,** PhD, ATR, author, artist, art therapist and teacher . . . . Page III

INDEX OF COLOUR PLATES